To:

_____

From:

_____

Date:

_____

© 2010 Summerside Press™
Minneapolis 55438
www.summersidepress.com

PROMISES & BLESSINGS
FOR A WOMAN'S HEART

A *Pocket Inspirations* Book

ISBN 978-1-60936-029-0

Scripture references are from the following sources: The Holy Bible, New
International Version®, NIV®. Copyright © 1973, 1978, 1984 by Biblica,
Inc.™ Used by permission of Zondervan. All rights reserved worldwide.
The New King James Version (NKJV). Copyright © 1982 by Thomas
Nelson, Inc. Used by permission. The Holy Bible, New Living Translation
(NLT). Copyright © 1996, 2004. Used by permission of Tyndale House
Publishers, Inc., Wheaton, Illinois 60189. *The Message* (MSG) © 1993,
1994, 1995, 1996, 2000, 2001, 2002 by Eugene Peterson. Used by
permission of NavPress, Colorado Springs, CO. The New Century Version®
(NCV). Copyright © 1987, 1988, 1991 by Thomas Nelson, Inc. Used by
permission. All rights reserved.

Excluding Scripture verses and deity pronouns, in some quotations references
to men and masculine pronouns have been replaced with gender-neutral
or feminine references. Additionally, in some quotations we have carefully
updated verb forms and wording that may distract modern readers.

Compiled by Barbara Farmer
Designed by Lisa & Jeff Franke

*Summerside Press™ is an inspirational publisher offering fresh,
irresistible books to uplift the heart and engage the mind.*

Printed in the USA.

PROMISES & BLESSINGS

FOR A

Woman's

HEART

summerside
PRESS

Woman of Beauty

For attractive lips,
Speak words of kindness.
For lovely eyes,
Seek out the good in people.
For a slim figure,
Share your food with the hungry.
For beautiful hair,
Let a child run his or her fingers through it once a day.
For poise,
Walk with the knowledge you'll never walk alone.

AUDREY HEPBURN

A woman of beauty...knows in her quiet center
where God dwells that He finds her beautiful,
and deemed her worthy, and in Him, she is enough.

JOHN AND STASI ELDREDGE

Taking joy in life
is a woman's best cosmetic.

ROSALIND RUSSELL

As a countenance is made beautiful by the soul's
shining through it, so the world is beautiful
by the shining through it of God.

FRIEDRICH HEINRICH JACOBI

It was Christ who discovered and emphasized
the worth of a woman. It was Christ who lifted her
into equality with man. It was Christ who gave
woman her chance, who saw her possibilities,
who discovered her value.

ARTHUR JOHN GOSSIP

....

*You should clothe yourselves...with the
beauty that comes from within,
the unfading beauty of a
gentle and quiet spirit,
which is so precious to God.*

1 PETER 3:4 NLT

....

A Centered Life

Life from the Center is a life of unhurried peace
and power. It is simple. It is serene.... We need not
get frantic. He is at the helm. And when our little day
is done, we lie down quietly in peace, for all is well.

THOMAS R. KELLY

Because we are spiritual beings...it is for our good,
individually and collectively, to live our lives
in interactive dependence upon God.

DALLAS WILLARD

Faith in God gives your life a center
from which you can reach out
and dare to love the world.

BARBARA FARMER

The center of power is not to be found in summit meetings or in peace conferences. It is not in Beijing or Washington or the United Nations, but rather where a child of God prays in the power of the Spirit for God's will to be done in her life, in her home, and in the world about her.

RUTH BELL GRAHAM

There is nothing but God's grace.
We walk upon it; we breathe it;
we live and die by it; it makes the
nails and axles of the universe.

ROBERT LOUIS STEVENSON

For in him we live and move and have our being.

ACTS 17:28 NIV

Always There

God is the sunshine that warms us, the rain
that melts the frost and waters the young plants.
The presence of God is a climate of strong
and bracing love, always there.

JOAN ARNOLD

Nothing we can do will make the Father love us less;
nothing we do can make Him love us more.
He loves us unconditionally with an everlasting love.
All He asks of us is that we respond to Him
with the free will that He has given to us.

NANCIE CARMICHAEL

The Creator thinks enough of you to have sent
Someone very special so that you might have life—
abundantly, joyfully, completely, and victoriously.

Tuck [this] thought into your heart today.
Treasure it. Your Father God cares about
your daily everythings that concern you.

KAY ARTHUR

The God who created, names, and numbers the stars
in the heavens also numbers the hairs of my head....
He pays attention to very big things
and to very small ones. What matters to me
matters to Him, and that changes my life.

ELISABETH ELLIOT

Whoever walks toward God one step,
God runs toward him two.

JEWISH PROVERB

....

*The LORD always keeps his promises;
he is gracious in all he does.*

PSALM 145:13 NLT

....

You Are the Miracle

I think miracles exist in part as gifts
and in part as clues that there is something
beyond the flat world we see.

PEGGY NOONAN

The miracles of nature do not seem
miracles because they are so common.
If no one had ever seen a flower,
even a dandelion would be the most
startling event in the world.

Face your deficiencies and acknowledge them;
but do not let them master you.
Let them teach you patience, sweetness, insight.
When we do the best we can, we never know
what miracle is wrought in our life,
or in the life of another.

HELEN KELLER

In the presence of hope—faith is born.
In the presence of faith—love becomes a possibility!
In the presence of love—miracles happen!

ROBERT SCHULLER

Do not pray for easy lives. Pray to be stronger....
Do not pray for tasks equal to your powers.
Pray for powers equal to your tasks.
Then the doing of your work shall be no miracle,
but you shall be the miracle.

PHILLIPS BROOKS

....

*It is clear to us, friends, that God not only
loves you very much but also has put
his hand on you for something special.*

1 THESSALONIANS 1:4 MSG

....

Daughter of the King

God is every moment totally aware
of each one of us. Totally aware in intense
concentration and love.... No one passes
through any area of life, happy or tragic,
without the attention of God.

EUGENIA PRICE

I need not lack now any more
For any lovely thing;
I need to know my birthright for
My Father is the King!

EVELYN GAGE

God is a rich and bountiful Father,
and He does not forget His children,
nor withhold from them anything which
it would be to their advantage to receive.

J. K. MACLEAN

We do not need to search for heaven,
over here or over there, in order to find
our eternal Father. In fact, we do not even need
to speak out loud, for though we speak in the
smallest whisper or the most fleeting thought,
He is close enough to hear us.

TERESA OF AVILA

Before anything else, above all else,
beyond everything else, God loves us.
God loves us extravagantly, ridiculously,
without limit or condition. God is
in love with us...God yearns for us.

ROBERTA BONDI

. . . .

*See how very much our Father loves us,
for he calls us his children, and that is what we are!*

1 JOHN 3:1 NLT

. . . .

Future Dreams

Allow your dreams a place in your prayers
and plans. God-given dreams can help you move
into the future He is preparing for you.

BARBARA JOHNSON

There is a past which is gone forever,
but there is a future which is still our own.

F. W. ROBERTSON

How could I be anything but quite happy
if I believed always that all the past is forgiven,
and all the present furnished with power,
and all the future bright with hope.

JAMES SMETHAM

HOPE is the ability to hear the music of the future....
FAITH is having the courage to dance to it today.

PETER KUZMIČ

Make the least of all that goes and the most
of all that comes. Don't regret what is past.
Cherish what you have. Look forward
to all that is to come. And most important of all,
rely moment by moment on Jesus Christ.

GIGI GRAHAM TCHIVIDJIAN

God has designs on our future...and He has
designed us for the future. He has given us something
to do in the future that no one else can do.

RUTH SENTER

....

*Delight yourself in the LORD
and he will give you
the desires of your heart.*

PSALM 37:4 NIV

....

Take Time

It may seem strange to think that God wants to
spend time with us, but...think about it.
If God went to all the trouble to come to earth,
to live the life that He did, to die for us,
then there's got to be a hunger and a passion
behind that. We think of prayer as an "ought to,"
but in reality it is a response to God's passionate
love for us. We need to refocus on the fact that God
is waiting for us to show up and be with Him
and that our presence truly touches Him.

DR. HENRY CLOUD

Life in the presence of God should be known
to us in conscious experience. It is a life
to be enjoyed every moment of every day.

A. W. TOZER

Intimacy may not be rushed.... We can't
dash into God's presence and choke down
spiritual inwardness.... [It] is
time-consuming, open only to minds
willing to sample spirituality in
small bites, savoring each one.

CALVIN MILLER

Come and sit and ask Him whatever is on
your heart. No question is too small, no riddle
too simple. He has all the time in the world.
Come and seek the will of God.

MAX LUCADO

....

*I've loved you the way my Father has loved me.
Make yourselves at home in my love.*

JOHN 15:9 MSG

....

Loving Others

Love is extravagant in the price it is willing to pay,
the time it is willing to give,
the hardships it is willing to endure,
and the strength it is willing to spend.

JONI EARECKSON TADA

Oh, if we did but love others! How easily
the least thing, the shutting of a door gently,
the walking softly, speaking low, not making
a noise, or the choice of a seat, so as to
leave the most convenient to others,
might become occasions of its exercise.

MÈRE ANGÉLIQUE ARNAULD

Love doesn't try to see through others,
but to see others through.

Trying to find yourself within yourself is like peeling the layers off an onion. When you finish you have nothing but a pile of peelings. The only way to find yourself is to go outside of yourself and love another.

RHONDA S. HOGAN

The reason we can dare to risk loving others is that "God has for Christ's sake loved us." Think of it! We are loved eternally, totally, individually, unreservedly! Nothing can take God's love away.

GLORIA GAITHER

....

Love...bears all things, believes all things, hopes all things, endures all things. Love never fails.

1 CORINTHIANS 13:4, 7–8 NKJV

....

God's Call to Us

In waiting we begin to get in touch with the
rhythms of life—stillness and action,
listening and decision. They are the rhythms
of God. It is in the everyday and the commonplace
that we learn patience, acceptance, and contentment.

RICHARD J. FOSTER

Know by the light of faith that
God is present, and be content with
directing all your actions toward Him.

BROTHER LAWRENCE

The Most High calls to us and waits for us
to respond. He desires to quench our deepest thirst,
to satisfy our deepest hunger, and to fill us with
His power and presence as we dwell in
the secret place of the Most High.

CYNTHIA HEALD

That is God's call to us—simply to be
people who are content to live close to Him
and to renew the kind of life in which
the closeness is felt and experienced.

THOMAS MERTON

Jesus is always waiting for us in silence.
In that silence, He will listen to us,
there He will speak to our soul,
and there we will hear His voice.

MOTHER TERESA

Our fulfillment comes in knowing God's glory,
loving Him for it, and delighting in it.

. . . .

The LORD longs to be gracious to you;
he rises to show you compassion.
Blessed are all those who wait for him.

ISAIAH 30:18 NIV

. . . .

You Have a Gift

We all have different gifts,
each of which came because of the grace
God gave us.... Anyone who has the gift of
serving should serve. Anyone who has the gift of
teaching should teach. Whoever has the gift of
encouraging others should encourage.
Whoever has the gift of giving to others
should give freely. Anyone who has the gift of
being a leader should try hard when he leads.
Whoever has the gift of showing mercy
to others should do so with joy.

ROMANS 12:6–8 NCV

If your lips can speak a word of encouragement
to a weary soul, you have a talent.

EVA J. CUMMINGS

As women, we want to know we are important
and that we have a significant place in our world.
We need to know that we matter to someone,
that our lives are making a difference
in the lives of other people,
that we are able to touch their souls.
This desire to have value is God-given.

BEVERLY LaHaye

Every one has a gift for something,
even if it is the gift of being a good friend.

MARIAN ANDERSON

....

*God has given each of you a gift from
his great variety of spiritual gifts.
Use them well to serve one another.*

1 PETER 4:10 NLT

....

Praise for the Day

Being grateful for what we have today
doesn't mean we have to have that forever.
It means we acknowledge that what we have today
is what we're supposed to have today.
There is enough.... And all we need will come to us.

MELODY BEATTIE

Our thanksgiving today should include those
things which we take for granted, and we
should continually praise our God, who is
true to His promise, who has provided
and retained the necessities for our living.

BETTY FUHRMAN

Thanksgiving puts power in living, because it
opens the generators of the heart to respond gratefully,
to receive joyfully, and to react creatively.

Thank You, God, for little things
That often come our way,
The things we take for granted
But don't mention when we pray.
The unexpected courtesy,
The thoughtful kindly deed,
A hand reached out to help us
In the time of sudden need.
Oh, make us more aware, dear God,
Of little daily graces
That come to us with sweet surprise
From never-dreamed-of places.

. . . .

*It is good to give thanks to the LORD,
And to sing praises to Your name, O Most High.*

PSALM 92:1 NKJV

. . . .

More than Skin Deep

We do not want merely to see beauty,
though, God knows, even that is bounty enough.
We want something else which can hardly be
put into words—to be united with the beauty we see,
to pass into it, to receive it into ourselves.

C. S. LEWIS

Virtue is to beauty what fragrance is to a flower.

All the flowers God has made are beautiful.
The rose in its glory and the lily in its whiteness
do not rob the tiny violet of its sweet smell,
or the daisy of its charming simplicity.

THÉRÈSE OF LISIEUX

The beautiful! It is beauty seen
with the eye of the soul.

JOSEPH JOUBERT

Virtue shows quite as well in rags and patches
as she does in purple and fine linen.

CHARLES DICKENS

Notice words of compassion.
Seek out deeds of kindness.
These are like the doves from heaven,
pointing out to you who are the ones blessed
with inner grace and beauty.

CHRISTOPHER DE VINCK

Life is what we are alive to. It is not length
but breadth.... Be alive to...goodness, kindness,
purity, love, history, poetry, music,
flowers, stars, God, and eternal hope.

MALTBIE D. BABCOCK

. . . .

*Charm is deceptive, and beauty
does not last; but a woman who
fears the LORD will be greatly praised.*

PROVERBS 31:30 NLT

. . . .

A Treasury of Faith

Within each of us there is an inner place
where the living God Himself longs to dwell,
our sacred center of belief.

There is no unbelief;
Whoever plants a seed beneath the sod
And waits to see it push away the clod,
She trusts in God.

ELIZABETH YORK CASE

I took an inventory and looked
into my little bag to see
what I had left over. I had one jewel left in the bag,
the brightest jewel of all. I had the gift of faith.

LOLA FALANA

I believe in the sun even if it isn't shining.
I believe in love even when I am alone.
I believe in God even when He is silent.

You are a child of your heavenly Father.
Confide in Him. Your faith in His love and power
can never be bold enough.

BASILEA SCHLINK

The soft, sweet summer was warm and glowing,
Bright were the blossoms on every bough:
I trusted Him when the roses were blooming;
I trust Him now....

L. B. COWMAN

. . . .

*Now faith is the substance of things hoped for,
the evidence of things not seen.*

HEBREWS 11:1 NKJV

. . . .

Family Memories

Sooner or later we all discover that the important
moments in life are not the advertised ones,
not the birthdays, the graduations, the weddings,
not the great goals achieved.
The real milestones are less prepossessing.
They come to the door of memory.

SUSAN B. ANTHONY

Family is of the utmost importance to me.
But my family is no more perfect than [any other]....
We love, trust, get hurt, sometimes outraged,
and we love and trust anyhow,
because that's the best way to let our love grow.

MADELEINE L'ENGLE

Families give us many things—love and meaning,
purpose and an opportunity to give,
and a sense of humor.

We were a strange little band of characters,
trudging through life sharing diseases
and toothpaste, coveting one another's desserts,
hiding shampoo, borrowing money,
locking each other out of our rooms,
inflicting pain and kissing to heal
it in the same instant,
loving, laughing, defending, and trying to figure out
the common thread that bound us all together.

ERMA BOMBECK

When you look at your life, the greatest
happinesses are family happinesses.

JOYCE BROTHERS

....

Finally, all of you should be in agreement,
understanding each other, loving each other
as family, being kind and humble.

1 PETER 3:8 NCV

....

Wait for the Promises

Peace does not dwell in outward things
but in the heart prepared to wait trustfully
and quietly on Him who has all things safely in
His hands.... Jesus had perfect trust in His Father,
whose will He had come to accomplish. Nothing
touched Him without His Father's permission.
Nothing touches me without my Father's
permission. Can I not then wait patiently?
He will show the way.

ELISABETH ELLIOT

A wise gardener plants her seeds,
then has the good sense not to dig them up
every few days to see if a crop is on the way.
Likewise, we must be patient as God brings
the answers...in His own good time.

QUIN SHERRER

We must wait for God, long, meekly, in the wind
and wet, in the thunder and lightning, in the
cold and the dark. Wait, and He will come.

FREDERICK W. FABER

The way may at times seem dark,
but light will arise, if you trust in the Lord,
and wait patiently for Him.

ELIZABETH T. KING

You are a little less than angels,
crown of creation, image of God.
Each person is a revelation, a transfiguration,
a waiting for Him to manifest Himself.

EDWARD FARRELL

....

*The Scriptures give us hope...as we wait
patiently for God's promises to be fulfilled.*

ROMANS 15:4 NLT

....

The Simple Things

Into all our lives, in many simple, familiar,
homely ways, God infuses this element of joy
from the surprises of life, which unexpectedly
brighten our days, and fill our eyes with light.

SAMUEL LONGFELLOW

We encounter God in the ordinariness of life,
not in the search for spiritual highs and
extraordinary, mystical experiences,
but in our simple presence in life.

BRENNAN MANNING

Living simply means concentrating on
what's important in light of eternity,
and not taking the rest of life too seriously.

ANNIE CHAPMAN

Happy people...enjoy the fundamental,
often very simple things of life....
They savor the moment, glad to be alive,
enjoying their work, their families, the good
things around them. They are adaptable;
they can bend with the wind.... Their eyes are
turned outward; they are aware, compassionate.
They have the capacity to love.

JANE CANFIELD

A crowded life leaves no space and no time for
enjoyment. Crowding distracts the mind, dulls the
senses, and starves the soul. Simplicity enriches.

DAVID YOUNT

....

*A devout life does bring wealth, but it's the
rich simplicity of being yourself before God.*

1 TIMOTHY 6:6 MSG

....

Moments to Reflect

Just as a prism of glass miters light and
casts a colored braid, a garden sings sweet
incantations the human heart strains to hear.
Hiding in every flower, in every leaf,
in every twig and bough, are reflections of
the God who once walked with us in Eden.

TONIA TRIEBWASSER

Reflection...enables our minds to be stretched
in three different directions—the direction that
leads to a proper relationship with God, the
relationship that leads to a healthy relationship
with others, and the relationship that leads to
a deeper understanding of oneself.

MARK CONNOLLY

Much of what is sacred is hidden in the ordinary,
everyday moments of our lives. To see something
of the sacred in those moments takes slowing
down so we can live our lives more reflectively.

KEN GIRE

What we lack is not so much leisure to do
as time to reflect and time to feel. What we
seldom "take" is time to experience the things
that have happened, the things that are happening,
the things that are still ahead of us.

MARGARET MEAD AND RHODA METRAUX

....

*Reflect on what I am saying, for the
Lord will give you insight into all this.*

2 TIMOTHY 2:7 NIV

....

Encouraging Hearts

When we take time to notice the simple things in life,
we never lack for encouragement.
We discover we are surrounded by a limitless hope
that's just wearing everyday clothes.

WENDY MOORE

Encouragement is being a good listener,
being positive, letting others know you accept them
for who they are. It is offering hope,
caring about the feelings of another, understanding.

GIGI GRAHAM TCHIVIDJIAN

Everyone has inside himself a piece of good news!
The good news is that you really don't know
how great you can be, how much you can love,
what you can accomplish and what your potential is.

ANNE FRANK

A word of encouragement to those we meet,
a cheerful smile in the supermarket,
a card or letter to a friend, a readiness to
witness when opportunity is given—
all are practical ways in which we may
let His light shine through us.

ELIZABETH B. JONES

There are times when encouragement means
such a lot. And a word is enough to convey it.

GRACE STRICKER DAWSON

....

*For we have great joy and consolation
in your love, because the hearts of the saints
have been refreshed by you.*

PHILEMON 1:7 NKJV

....

God's Tender Love

Open your hearts to the love God instills....
God loves you tenderly. What He gives you is not
to be kept under lock and key, but to be shared.

MOTHER TERESA

There is no need to plead that the love of God
shall fill our hearts as though He were unwilling
to fill us.... Love is pressing around us on all sides
like air. Cease to resist it and instantly
love takes possession.

AMY CARMICHAEL

Nothing can separate you from His love,
absolutely nothing.... God is enough for time,
and God is enough for eternity.
God is enough!

HANNAH WHITALL SMITH

In God's wisdom, He frequently chooses
to meet our needs by showing His love toward us
through the hands and hearts of others.

JACK HAYFORD

Love has its source in God, for love
is the very essence of His being.

KAY ARTHUR

God is changeless. He will be unusual.
He won't strike an average anywhere.
He will get out of bounds and meet us on any level
with His patience and His love and His bounty.

JEAN CHURCH

. . . .

You gave me life and
showed me your unfailing love.
My life was preserved by your care.

JOB 10:12 NLT

. . . .

Blessings Await

We walk without fear, full of hope
and courage and strength to do His will,
waiting for the endless good which He is
always giving as fast as He can
get us able to take it in.

GEORGE MACDONALD

God is waiting for us to come to Him
with our needs.... God's throne room is
always open.... Every single believer
in the whole world could walk into
the throne room all at one time, and it
would not even be crowded.

CHARLES STANLEY

See Jesus in everything and
in everything you will find blessing.

You are never alone. In your heart of hearts,
in the place where no two people are ever alike,
Christ is waiting for you. And what you
never dared hope for springs to life.

ROGER OF TAIZÉ

God wants us to look to Jesus,
the author and finisher of our faith.
He has already overcome similar trials and
tribulations and will give us the power
to do the same. He waits only to be asked.

BILLY GRAHAM

....

*The blessings God has for his children...
which cannot be destroyed or be spoiled or lose
their beauty, are kept in heaven for you.*

1 PETER 1:4 NCV

....

Soul Satisfying

To be glad of life, because it gives you the
chance to love and to work and to play and to
look up at the stars; to be satisfied with your
possessions, but not contented with yourself
until you have made the best of them;...
to think seldom of your enemies,
often of your friends, and every day of Christ;
and to spend as much time as you can,
with body and with spirit in God's
out-of-doors—these are little guideposts
on the footpath to peace.

HENRY VAN DYKE

True contentment is a real, even an active,
virtue—not only affirmative but creative.
It is the power of getting out of any
situation all there is in it.

G. K. CHESTERTON

Life is not intended to be simply a round
of work, no matter how interesting and
important that work may be. A moment's pause
to watch the glory of a sunrise or a sunset is
soul satisfying, while a bird's song will
set the steps to music all day long.

LAURA INGALLS WILDER

To love is to be content with the present moment,
open to its meaning, entering into its mystery.

ELIZABETH O'CONNOR

....

*Satisfy us in the morning with
your unfailing love, that we may sing
for joy and be glad all our days.*

PSALM 90:14 NIV

....

Embracing Love

Sooner or later we begin to understand
that love is more than verses on valentines
and romance in the movies. We begin to know
that love is here and now, real and true,
the most important thing in our lives.
For love is the creator of our favorite memories
and the foundation of our fondest dreams.
Love is a promise that is always kept,
a fortune that can never be spent,
a seed that can flourish in even the most
unlikely of places. And this radiance that
never fades, this mysterious and magical joy,
is the greatest treasure of all—
one known only by those who love.

The treasure our heart searches for is
found in the ocean of God's love.

JANET L. SMITH

Though I have seen the oceans and mountains,
though I have read great books and seen
great works of art, though I have heard symphonies
and tasted the best wines and foods,
there is nothing greater or more beautiful
than those people I love.

CHRISTOPHER DE VINCK

Is life not full of opportunities for learning love?...
The world is not a playground, it is a schoolroom.
Life is not a holiday, but an education.
And the one eternal lesson for us all
is how better we can love.

HENRY DRUMMOND

....

Three things will last forever—
faith, hope, and love—
and the greatest of these is love.

1 CORINTHIANS 13:13 NLT

....

Work of Art

She is the crescendo, the final, astonishing
work of God. Woman. In one last flourish
creation comes to a finish not with Adam,
but with *Eve*. She is the Master's finishing touch.

JOHN AND STASI ELDREDGE

Then the LORD God made a woman from the rib,
and he brought her to the man.
"At last!" the man exclaimed. "This one is
bone from my bone, and flesh from my flesh!"

GENESIS 2:22–23 NLT

You are a creation of God unequaled anywhere
in the universe.... Thank Him for yourself and then
for all the rest of His glorious handiwork.

NORMAN VINCENT PEALE

Each one of us is God's special work of art. Through us, He teaches and inspires, delights and encourages, informs and uplifts all those who view our lives. God, the master artist, is most concerned about expressing himself— His thoughts and His intentions—through what He paints in our character.... [He] wants to paint a beautiful portrait of His Son in and through your life. A painting like no other in all of time.

JONI EARECKSON TADA

. . . .

I praise you because I am fearfully and wonderfully made; your works are wonderful, I know that full well.

PSALM 139:14 NIV

. . . .

Audience of One

We need quiet time to examine our lives
openly and honestly...spending quiet time
alone gives your mind an opportunity to
renew itself and create order.

SUSAN L. TAYLOR

Solitude liberates us from entanglements by
carving out a space from which we can see ourselves
and our situation before the Audience of One.
Solitude provides the private place where we can
take our bearings and so make God our North Star.

OS GUINNESS

We receive only when we are recollected; only in
silence is heard the beating of the heart of God.

BERNARDO OLIVERA

Solitude begins with a time and place for God, and God alone. If we really believe not only that God exists but also that He is actively present in our lives—healing, teaching, guiding— we need to set aside a time and space to give Him our undivided attention.

HENRI J. M. NOUWEN

Time passed in silence with God is time spent growing in relationship with Him. And time spent letting His love flow through you to others is an investment in eternity.

AMY AND JUDGE REINHOLD

. . . .

When you pray, go away by yourself...and pray to your Father in private. Then your Father, who sees everything, will reward you.

MATTHEW 6:6 NLT

. . . .

A Kiss from Heaven

Some days, it is enough encouragement just to watch
the clouds break up and disappear, leaving behind
a blue patch of sky and bright sunshine that is
so warm upon my face. It's a glimpse of divinity;
a kiss from heaven.

We are so preciously loved by God that
we cannot even comprehend it. No created being
can ever know how much and how sweetly
and tenderly God loves them.

JULIAN OF NORWICH

God makes our lives a medley of joy and tears,
hope and help, love and encouragement.

God created us with an overwhelming desire to soar.
Our desire to develop and use every ounce of
potential He's placed in us is not egotistical.
He designed us to be tremendously productive
and "to mount up with wings like eagles,"
realistically dreaming of what
He can do with our potential.

CAROL KENT

You are in the Beloved...therefore infinitely dear
to the Father, unspeakably precious to Him.
You are never, not for one second, alone.

NORMAN DOWTY

....

*May our Lord Jesus Christ himself and God
our Father encourage you and strengthen you
in every good thing you do and say.*

2 THESSALONIANS 2:16 NCV

....

He's Thinking of You

Heaven knows no difference between Sunday
morning and Wednesday afternoon. God longs to
speak as clearly in the workplace as He does in
the sanctuary. He longs to be worshiped when
we sit at the dinner table and not just when we come
to His communion table.... There's never a moment
when He's not thinking of you.

MAX LUCADO

We need never shout across the spaces to
an absent God. He is nearer than our own soul,
closer than our most secret thoughts.

A. W. TOZER

Are not two sparrows sold for a penny? Yet
not one of them will fall to the ground apart from
the will of your Father.... So don't be afraid; you are
worth more than many sparrows.

MATTHEW 10:29, 31 NIV

Almighty, most holy, most high God,
thank You for paying attention to small things.
Thank You for valuing the insignificant.
Thank You for being interested in the lilies of
the field and the birds of the air.
Thank You far caring about me. Amen.

RICHARD J. FOSTER

We have been in God's thought from all
eternity, and in His creative love,
His attention never leaves us.

MICHAEL QUOIST

....

*How precious are your
thoughts about me, O God.
They cannot be numbered!*

PSALM 139:17 NLT

....

We Need Each Other

Loving and being loved is the greatest of
human joys, the ultimate human experience.
We can exist without love; but we are not
living fully as human beings without it.

EDWARD E. FORD

I feel from a spiritual standpoint that there's a real
celebration of humanity, of the common bond
of everybody. We need each other.

AMY GRANT

More and more I realize that everybody,
regardless of age, needs to be hugged and comforted
in a brotherly or sisterly way now and then.
Preferably now.

JANE HOWARD

Love allows us to live,
and through living we grow in loving.

EVELYN MANDEL

Sometimes in those around me
With burdens, hurts and fears:
Through joyful, happy hours
And often through their tears:
In some loving act of kindness
As they show how much they care—
In the lives of folk around me
I find God reflected there.

CYRUS E. ALBERTSON

We really need only five things on this earth:
Some food, some sun, some work,
some fun, and someone.

BEATRICE NOLAN

The greatest gift we can give one another is
rapt attention to one another's existence.

SUE ATCHLEY EBAUGH

....

*Love each other with genuine affection,
and take delight in honoring each other.*

ROMANS 12:10 NLT

....

Look for Joy

Each day is a treasure box of gifts from God,
just waiting to be opened. Open your gifts
with excitement. You will find forgiveness
attached to ribbons of joy. You will find
love wrapped in sparkling gems.

JOAN CLAYTON

With God, life is eternal—both in quality and length.
There is no joy comparable to the joy of discovering
something new from God, about
God. If the continuing
life is a life of joy, we will go on discovering, learning.

EUGENIA PRICE

Happiness comes of the capacity to feel deeply,
to enjoy simply, to think freely,
to risk life, to be needed.

STORM JAMESON

A joyful heart is like a sunshine of God's love,
the hope of eternal happiness, a
burning flame of God....
And if we pray, we will become that sunshine
of God's love—in our own home, the place
where we live, and in the world at large.

MOTHER TERESA

You have to *look* for the joy.
Look for the light of God that is hitting your life,
and you will find sparkles you didn't know were there.

BARBARA JOHNSON

....

All who seek the LORD will praise him.
Their hearts will rejoice with everlasting joy.

PSALM 22:26 NLT

....

God Our Father

People who don't know God and the way
he works fuss over these things, but you know
both God and how he works. Steep yourself
in God-reality, God-initiative, God-provisions.
You'll find all your everyday human concerns
will be met. Don't be afraid of missing out.
You're my dearest friends! The Father wants to
give you the very kingdom itself.

LUKE 12:30–32 MSG

If God, like a father, denies us
what we want now, it is in order to give us
some far better thing later on.
The will of God, we can rest assured,
is invariably a better thing.

ELISABETH ELLIOT

From the tiny birds of the air and from the fragile lilies of the field we learn the same truth, which is so important for those who desire a life of simple faith: God takes care of His own. He knows our needs. He anticipates our crises. He is moved by our weaknesses. He stands ready to come to our rescue. And at just the right moment He steps in and proves Himself as our faithful heavenly Father.

CHARLES SWINDOLL

Ps. 145:8-9

If nothing seems to go my way today,
this is my happiness: God is my Father
and I am His child.

BASILEA SCHLINK

....

*God is the Father who is
full of mercy and all comfort.*

2 CORINTHIANS 1:3 NCV

....

Time To Be

Time is a very precious gift of God;
so precious that it's only given to us
moment by moment.

AMELIA BARR

See each morning a world made anew,
as if it were the morning of the very first day;...
treasure and use it, as if it were
the final hour of the very last day.

FAY HARTZELL ARNOLD

Take time to notice all the usually unnoticed,
simple things in life. Delight in the never-ending
hope that's available every day!

We need time to dream, time to remember,
and time to reach the infinite.
Time to be.

GLADYS TABER

At the end of your life you will never regret
not having passed one more test, not winning one
more verdict, or not closing one more deal.
You will regret time not spent with
a husband, a friend, a child, or a parent.

BARBARA BUSH

Live your life while you have it.
Life is a splendid gift—
there is nothing small about it.

FLORENCE NIGHTINGALE

Life varies its stories. Time changes
everything, yet what is truly valuable—
what is worth keeping—is beyond time.

RUTH SENTER

....

*Live well, live wisely, live humbly.
It's the way you live, not the
way you talk, that counts.*

JAMES 3:16 MSG

....

Beyond Description

Experience God in the breathless wonder
and startling beauty that is all around you.
His sun shines warm upon your face.
His wind whispers in the treetops.
Like the first rays of morning light,
celebrate the start of each day with God.

WENDY MOORE

The beauty of the earth, the beauty of the sky,
the order of the stars, the sun, the moon...
their very loveliness is their confession of God:
for who made these lovely mutable things,
but He who is Himself unchangeable beauty?

AUGUSTINE

Something deep in all of us yearns for God's beauty,
and we can find it no matter where we are.

SUE MONK KIDD

Beauty born of beauty breeds beauty in every way....
A person who is given words of beauty
is a person who will express beauty....
All beauty can be traced, ultimately, to God.

CHRISTOPHER DE VINCK

You are beautiful beyond description, [Lord,]
Too marvelous for words;
Too wonderful of comprehension,
Like nothing ever seen or heard.
Who can grasp Your infinite wisdom?
Who can fathom the depth of Your love?
You are beautiful beyond description,
Majesty enthroned above.

BOB FITTS

....

*Holy, holy, holy is the LORD of hosts;
The whole earth is full of His glory!*

ISAIAH 6:3 NKJV

....

A Quiet Spirit

Year by year the complexities of this
spinning world grow more bewildering,
and so each year we need all the more to
seek peace and comfort in the joyful simplicities.

In a world where it is necessary to succeed,
perhaps...we women know more deeply
that success can be a quiet and hidden thing.

PAM BROWN

Don't ever let yourself get so busy that you
miss those little but important extras in life—
the beauty of a day...the smile of a friend...
the serenity of a quiet moment alone.
For it is often life's smallest pleasures and
gentlest joys that make the biggest
and most lasting difference.

A quiet place is a good place to find out
God's angle on any problem.

JANETTE OKE

Calm me, O Lord, as You stilled the storm,
Still me, O Lord, keep me from harm.
Let all the tumult within me cease,
Enfold me, Lord, in Your peace.

CELTIC TRADITIONAL

Quiet is good. Peace is an invaluable commodity
one can never get too much of.

....

He makes me lie down in green pastures,
he leads me beside quiet waters,
he restores my soul.

PSALM 23:2–3 NIV

....

The Beauty of Truth

God who is goodness and truth is also beauty.
It is this innate human and divine longing,
found in the company of goodness and truth,
that is able to recognize and leap up at beauty
and rejoice and know that all is beautiful,
that there is not one speck of beauty under the sun
that does not mirror back the beauty of God.

ROBERTA BONDI

The simplest and commonest truth seems
new and wonderful when we experience it
the first time in our own life.

MARIE VON EBNER-ESCHENBACH

Truth is such a rare thing,
it is delightful to tell it.

EMILY DICKINSON

It is an extraordinary and beautiful thing that God,
in creation...works with the beauty of matter;
the reality of things; the discoveries of the senses,
all five of them; so that we, in turn,
may hear the grass growing;
see a face springing to life in love and laughter....
The offerings of creation...our glimpses of truth.

MADELIENE L'ENGLE

I am amazed by the sayings of Christ.
They seem truer than anything I have ever read.
And they certainly turn the world upside down.

KATHERINE BUTLER HATHAWAY

. . . .

*Jesus said..., "If you abide in My word...
you shall know the truth, and the
truth shall make you free."*

JOHN 8:31–32 NKJV

. . . .

God's Abundance

Focus your full attention on the goodness
and greatness of your Father rather than on the
size of your need. Your need is so small
compared to His ability to meet it.

I think what we're longing for is not
"the good life" as it's been advertised to us...
but life in its fullness, its richness,
its abundance. Living more reflectively
helps us enter into that fullness.

KEN GIRE

His overflowing love delights
to make us partakers of the bounties
He graciously imparts.

HANNAH MORE

God's gifts make us truly wealthy.
His loving supply never shall leave us wanting.

BECKY LAIRD

Faith is the bucket of power lowered by the rope
of prayer into the well of God's abundance.
What we bring up depends upon what we let down.
We have every encouragement to use a big bucket.

VIRGINIA WHITMAN

The resource from which [God] gives is
boundless, measureless, unlimited, unending,
abundant, almighty, and eternal.

JACK HAYFORD

The Lord's chief desire is to reveal Himself
to you and, in order for Him to do that,
He gives you abundant grace.

MADAME JEANNE GUYON

....

*You, O Lord, are a compassionate and gracious God,
slow to anger, abounding in love and faithfulness.*

PSALM 86:15 NIV

....

A Fragrant Effect

The blossom cannot tell what becomes of
its fragrance as it drifts away, just as no person
can tell what becomes of her influence
as she continues through life.

This I learned from the shadow of a tree,
That to and fro did sway against a wall,
Our shadow selves, our influence, may fall
Where we ourselves can never be.

ANNA HAMILTON

There are two kinds of people in the world:
those who come into a room and say,
"Here I am!"
and those who come in and say,
"Ah, there you are!"

What we feel, think, and do this moment influences
both our present and the future in ways we may
never know. Begin. Start right where you are.
Consider your possibilities and find inspiration...
to add more meaning and zest to your life.

ALEXANDRA STODDARD

Many women...have buoyed me up in times of
weariness and stress. Each friend was important....
Their words have seasoned my life.
Influence, just like salt shaken out, is hard to see,
but its flavor is hard to miss.

PAM FARREL

. . . .

*Thanks be to God, who always leads us...in Christ
and through us spreads everywhere the
fragrance of the knowledge of him.*

2 CORINTHIANS 2:14 NIV

. . . .

Comfort of a Friend

I cannot count the number of times
I have been strengthened by another woman's
heartfelt hug, appreciative note, surprise gift,
or caring questions.... My friends are an oasis to me,
encouraging me to go on. They are
essential to my well-being.

DEE BRESTIN

Knowing what to say is not always necessary;
just the presence of a caring friend
can make a world of difference.

SHERI CURRY

A friend understands what you are trying to say...even
when your thoughts aren't fitting into words.

ANN D. PARRISH

What shall I bestow upon a friend?
Gay laughter to sustain when sorrow may bring pain,
a bright song of life, a belief that winter ends
in the glory of spring, and a prayer of hope
for peace that will forever stay.

LEA PALMER

A friend hears the song in my heart
and sings it to me when my memory fails.

Silences make the real conversations
between friends. Not the saying,
but the never needing to say is what counts.

MARGARET LEE RUNBECK

....

*Reliable friends who do what they say
are like cool drinks in sweltering heat—refreshing!*

PROVERBS 25:13 MSG

....

Sweet Contentment

You're blessed when you're content with just
who you are—no more, no less. That's the
moment you find yourselves proud owners
of everything that can't be bought.

MATTHEW 5:5 MSG

Love, consolation, and peace bloom only
in the garden of sweet contentment.

MARTHA ANDERSON

It is always wise to stop wishing for things
long enough to enjoy the fragrance
of those now flowering.

PATRICE GIFFORD

If we are cheerful and contented, all nature smiles...
the flowers are more fragrant, the birds sing more
sweetly, and the sun, moon, and stars all appear
more beautiful, and seem to rejoice with us.

ORISON SWETT MARDEN

I am still determined to be cheerful and happy,
in whatever situation I may be;
for I have also learned from experience
that the greater part of our happiness or misery
depends upon our dispositions,
and not upon our circumstances.

MARTHA WASHINGTON

Gratitude is the heart of contentment.
I have never met a truly thankful, appreciative
person who was not profoundly happy.

NEIL CLARK WARREN

Contentment is not the fulfillment of what you want,
but the realization of how much you already have.

. . . .

*If you're content to be simply yourself,
you will become more than yourself.*

LUKE 14:11 MSG

. . . .

Healing Laughter

A keen sense of humor helps us to overlook the unbecoming, understand the unconventional, tolerate the unpleasant, overcome the unexpected, and outlast the unbearable.

BILLY GRAHAM

Take time to laugh.
It is the music of the soul.

Laughter dulls the sharpest pain and flattens out the greatest stress. To share it is to give a gift of health because, as someone pointed out, "Ulcers can't grow while you're laughing."

HUNTER "PATCH" ADAMS

Laughing at ourselves as well as with each other gives a surprising sense of togetherness.

HAZEL C. LEE

The best laughter, the laughter that can heal,
the laughter that has the truest ring, is the laughter
that flowers out of a love for life and its Giver.

MAXINE HANCOCK

Whole-hearted, ready laughter heals, encourages,
relaxes anyone within hearing distance.
The laughter that springs from love makes
wide the space around—gives room for
the loved one to enter in.

EUGENIA PRICE

If you can learn to laugh in spite of
the circumstances that surround you,
you will enrich others, enrich yourself,
and more than that, you will last!

BARBARA JOHNSON

. . . .

*A cheerful look brings joy to the heart;
good news makes for good health.*

PROVERBS 15:30 NLT

. . . .

Blessings from Above

As you sit quietly in My presence remember
I am a God of abundance. I will never run out
of resources; My capacity to bless you is unlimited....
Through spending time in My presence,
you gain glimpses of My overflowing vastness.
These glimpses are tiny foretastes of what
you will experience eternally in heaven.
Even now you have access to as much of Me
as you have faith to receive. Rejoice in
my abundance—living by faith, not by sight.

SARAH YOUNG

Lift up your eyes.
Your heavenly Father waits to bless you—
in inconceivable ways to make your life
what you never dreamed it could be.

ANNE ORTLUND

How great is the goodness you have
stored up for those who fear you. You lavish it
on those who come to you for protection,
blessing them before the watching world.

PSALM 31:19 NLT

Strength, rest, guidance, grace, help,
sympathy, love—all from God to us!
What a list of blessings!

EVELYN STENBOCK

Have you ever thought that in every action
of grace in your heart you have the whole
omnipotence of God engaged to bless you?

ANDREW MURRAY

....

*When you grant a blessing, O LORD,
it is an eternal blessing!*

1 CHRONICLES 17:27 NLT

....

Beauty of the Earth

Those who contemplate the beauty of the earth find
reserves of strength that will endure as long as life lasts.
There is symbolic as well as actual beauty in the
migration of the birds, the ebb and flow of the tides,
the folded bud ready for the spring.
There is something infinitely healing in the
repeated refrains of nature—the assurance that
dawn comes after night, and spring after the winter.

RACHEL CARSON

The very act of planting a seed in the earth
has in it to me something beautiful.
I always do it with a joy
that is largely mixed with awe.

CELIA LAIGHTON THAXTER

There is beauty in the forest
When the trees are green and fair,
There is beauty in the meadow
When the wildflowers scent the air.
There is beauty in the sunlight
and the soft blue beams above.
Oh, the world is full of beauty
when the heart is full of love.

One cannot collect all the beautiful shells on
the beach. One can collect only a few,
and they are more beautiful if they are few.

ANNE MORROW LINDBERGH

. . . .

*Just as each day brims with your beauty,
my mouth brims with praise.*

PSALM 71:8 MSG

. . . .

Rest in the Lord

God provides resting places as well as
working places. Rest, then, and be thankful
when He brings you, wearied, to a wayside well.

L. B. COWMAN

Rest is not idleness, and to lie sometimes on
the grass under the trees on a summer's day,
listening to the murmur of water, or
watching the clouds float across the sky,
is by no means a waste of time.

SIR JOHN LUBBOCK

At times it is only necessary to rest oneself in
silence for a few minutes, in order to take off
the pressure and become wonderfully refreshed.

DRESSER

True silence is the rest of the mind;
it is to the spirit what sleep is to the body:
nourishment and refreshment.

WILLIAM PENN

Joy comes from knowing God loves me
and knows who I am and where I'm going...
that my future is secure as I rest in Him.

DR. JAMES DOBSON

A life of inward rest and outward victory is the
inalienable birthright of every child of God.

HANNAH WHITALL SMITH

. . . .

*Relax, everything's going to be all right;
rest, everything's coming together;
open your hearts, love is on the way!*

JUDE 1:2 MSG

. . . .

He Provides

God may not provide us with a perfectly
ordered life, but what He does provide is Himself,
His presence, and open doors that bring us closer
to being productive, positive, and realistic...women.

JUDITH BRILES

I must simply be thankful, and I am, for all
the Lord has provided for me, whether
big or small in the eyes of someone else.

MABEL P. ADAMSON

There will be days which are great and everything
goes as planned. There will be other days
when we aren't sure why we got out of bed.
Regardless of which kind of day it is, we can be
assured that God takes care of our daily needs.

EMILIE BARNES

You can trust God right now to supply all your needs for today. And if your needs are more tomorrow, His supply will be greater also.

A new path lies before us;
We're not sure where it leads;
But God goes on before us,
Providing all our needs.
This path, so new, so different
Exciting as we climb,
Will guide us in His perfect will
Until the end of time.

LINDA MAURICE

....

*God will generously provide all you need.
Then you will always have everything you need
and plenty left over to share with others.*

2 CORINTHIANS 9:8 NLT

....

Give Praise

I found the sun for me this morning.
I thank You, Lord. I found the warm water
in the shower. I praise You. I found the bread
in my kitchen this morning, Lord. I thank You.
I found the fresh air as I stood outside the door.
I praise You. For all that I see that You do for me,
I thank You. For all that I do not see
that You do for me, I praise You.

CHRISTOPHER DE VINCK

Let us give all that lies within us...
to pure praise, to pure loving adoration,
and to worship from a grateful heart—
a heart that is trained to look up.

AMY CARMICHAEL

Like supernatural effervescence,
praise will sometimes bubble up
from the joy of simply knowing Christ.
Praise like that is...delight. Pure pleasure!
But praise can also be supernatural determination.
A decisive action. Praise like that is...quiet resolve.
Fixed devotion. Strength of spirit.

JONI EARECKSON TADA

They that trust the Lord find
many things to praise Him for.
Praise follows trust.

LILY MAY GOULD

....

I will give thanks to the LORD because of
His righteousness and will sing praise
to the name of the LORD Most High.

PSALM 7:17 NIV

....

Serenity in Life

Over the margins of life comes a whisper,
a faint call, a premonition of richer living
which we know we are passing by.
Strained by the very mad pace of our daily
outer burdens, we are further strained by
an inward uneasiness, because we have hints
that there is a way of life vastly richer and
deeper than all this hurried existence, a life of
unhurried serenity and peace and power.

THOMAS R. KELLY

While both boredom and serenity
address the passage of time,
the former yawns and rolls its eyes,
the latter sighs and revels in its value.

BARBARA FARMER

Not every day of our lives is overflowing
with joy and celebration. But there are moments
when our hearts nearly burst within us for the
sheer joy of being alive. The first sight of
our newborn babies, the warmth of love
in another's eyes, the fresh scent of rain on
a hot summer's eve—moments like these
renew in us a heartfelt appreciation for life.

GWEN ELLIS

All those who live with any degree of serenity
live by some assurance of grace.

REINHOLD NIEBUHR

. . . .

*I pray that the God who gives hope will fill you
with much joy and peace while you trust in him.*

ROMANS 15:13 NCV

. . . .

In His Image

Whatever it means to bear God's image,
you do so *as a woman*. Female.
That's how and where you bear His image.
Your feminine heart has been created
with the greatest of all possible dignities—
as a reflection of God's own heart.

JOHN AND STASI ELDREDGE

I am convinced that God has built into all of us an
appreciation of beauty and has even allowed us to
participate in the creation of beautiful things
and places. It may be one way God brings healing
to our brokenness, and a way that we can contribute
toward bringing wholeness to our fallen world.

MARY JANE WORDEN

We must know that we have been created for
greater things, not just to be a number in the world,
not just to go for diplomas and degrees....
We have been created in order to love and to be loved.

MOTHER TERESA

You are God's created beauty and the focus
of His affection and delight.

JANET L. SMITH

....

So God created human beings in his own image.
In the image of God he created them;
male and female he created them.

GENESIS 1:27 NLT

....

An Invitation

Are you tired? Worn out? Burned out on religion?
Come to me. Get away with me and you'll recover
your life. I'll show you how to take a real rest.
Walk with me and work with me—watch how I do it.
Learn the unforced rhythms of grace. I won't
lay anything heavy or ill-fitting on you.
Keep company with me and you'll learn
to live freely and lightly.

MATTHEW 11:28–30 MSG

God says to His children: Are you lonesome?
Breathe out My name. Come to Me and I will be
your friend. Are you sick? Come to Me for healing.
Are you left out of things? Feeling rejected
and pushed aside? Come home to Me.

ALICE CHAPIN

[God] is looking for people who will come
in simple dependence upon His grace,
and rest in simple faith upon His greatness.
At this very moment, He's looking at you.

JACK HAYFORD

God wants us to be present where we are.
He invites us to see and to hear
what is around us and, through it all,
to discern the footprints of the Holy.

RICHARD J. FOSTER

. . . .

*Come with me by yourselves
to a quiet place and get some rest.*

MARK 6:31 NIV

. . . .

Gift of Truth

Every good action and every perfect gift is from God.
These good gifts come down from the Creator
of the sun, moon, and stars, who does not change
like their shifting shadows. God decided to give us
life through the word of truth so we might be
the most important of all the things He made.

JAMES 1:17–18 NCV

Amid ancient lore the Word of God
stands unique and pre-eminent.
Wonderful in its construction, admirable
in its adaptation, it contains truths that
a child may comprehend, and mysteries
into which angels desire to look.

FRANCES ELLEN WATKINS HARPER

The wonder of our Lord is that He is so accessible
to us in the common things of our lives:...
welcoming children into our arms...fellowship
over a meal...giving thanks. A simple attitude of
caring, listening, and lovingly telling the truth.

NANCIE CARMICHAEL

Open my eyes that I may see
Glimpses of truth Thou hast for me.
Place in my hands the wonderful key
That shall unclasp and set me free.

CLARA H. SCOTT

....

*Give yourselves to the gifts God gives you.
Most of all, try to proclaim his truth.*

1 CORINTHIANS 14:1 MSG

....

A Heart Full of Gratitude

Gratitude unlocks the fullness of life.
It turns what we have into enough, and more....
It can turn a meal into a feast, a house into a home,
a stranger into a friend. Gratitude makes sense
of our past, brings peace for today, and
creates a vision for tomorrow.

MELODY BEATTIE

Appreciation is like salt—a little goes a
long way to bring out the best in us.

Were there no God we would be
in this glorious world with grateful hearts
and no one to thank.

CHRISTINA ROSSETTI

To be grateful is to recognize the
love of God in everything He has given us—
and He has given us everything.
Every breath we draw is a gift of His love,
every moment of existence is a gift of grace.

THOMAS MERTON

Maybe we could spend a moment at the end
of each day and decide to remember that day—
whatever may have happened—as a day
to be grateful for. In so doing we increase our
heart's capacity to choose joy.

HENRI J. M. NOUWEN

....

*Give thanks to the LORD, for he is good!
His faithful love endures forever.*

1 CHRONICLES 16:34 NLT

....

At His Feet

Because God is responsible for our welfare,
we are told to cast all our care upon Him,
for He cares for us. God says, "I'll take the burden—
don't give it a thought—leave it to Me."
God is keenly aware that we are dependent
upon Him for life's necessities.

BILLY GRAHAM

We sometimes fear to bring our troubles to God,
because they must seem so small to Him
who sitteth on the circle of the earth. But if they are
large enough to vex and endanger our welfare,
they are large enough to touch His heart of love.

R. A. TORREY

It is such a comfort to drop the tangles of life
into God's hands and leave them there.

L. B. COWMAN

There is an activity of the spirit, silent, unseen,
which must be the dynamic of any form of truly
creative, fruitful trust. When we commit a
predicament, a possibility, a person to God
in genuine confidence, we do not merely step aside
and tap our foot until God comes through.
We remain involved. We remain in contact with God
in gratitude and praise. But we do this
without anxiety, without worry.

EUGENIA PRICE

....

*Give all your worries and cares to God,
for he cares about you.*

1 PETER 5:7 NLT

....

Girlfriends

There are some friends you know you will
have for the rest of your life. You're welded
together by love, trust, respect, loss—
or simple embarrassment.

We should all have one person who knows
how to bless us despite the evidence.

PHYLLIS THEROUX

A friend is one who laughs at your jokes
when they're not very funny and sympathizes with
your problems when they're not very serious.

Happiness is a friend who pulls the toilet paper
off your shoe before you make a big entrance.

The happiest business in all the world
is that of making friends,
And no investment on the street
pays larger dividends,
For life is more than stocks and bonds,
and love than rate percent,
And she who gives in friendship's name
shall reap what she has spent.

I am only as strong as the coffee I drink,
the hairspray I use, and the friends I have.

....

*This is my commandment: love one other in the
same way I have loved you. There is no greater love
than to lay down one's life for one's friends.*

JOHN 15:12–13 NLT

....

Priorities and Perspectives

Choices can change our lives profoundly.
The choice to mend a broken relationship,
to say yes to a difficult assignment,
to lay aside some important work to play
with a child, to visit some forgotten person—
these small choices may affect our lives eternally.

GLORIA GAITHER

Never let the urgent crowd out the important.

KELLY CATLIN WALKER

How you do something and the attitude
with which you do it are usually even more
important than what you do.... Often we have
no choice about doing things, but we can always
choose how to do them. And that...can make
all the difference in your daily life.

NORMAN VINCENT PEALE

We cannot rebuild the world by ourselves, but we can have a small part in it by beginning where we are. It may only be taking care of a neighbor's child or inviting someone to dinner, but it is important.

DONNA L. GLAZIER

The goal of much that is written about in life management is to enable us to do more in less time. But is this necessarily a desirable goal? Perhaps we need to get less done, but the right things.

JEAN FLEMING

....

Let's not get tired of doing what is good.... Therefore, whenever we have the opportunity, we should do good to everyone.

GALATIANS 6:9–10 NLT

....

God's Workmanship

Why did God give us imaginations?
Because they help unfold His kingdom.
Imagination unveils the Great Imaginer.
In the beginning, God created. He imagined
the world into being. Every flower, animal,
mountain, and rainbow is a product
of God's creative imagination.

JILL M. RICHARDSON

May God give you eyes to see beauty
only the heart can understand.

As God's workmanship, we deserve to be treated,
and to treat ourselves, with affection and affirmation,
regardless of our appearance or performance.

MARY ANN MAYO

The more I study nature, the more
I am amazed at the Creator.

LOUIS PASTEUR

God has a wonderful plan for each person
He has chosen. He knew even before He
created this world what beauty
He would bring forth from our lives.

LOUISE B. WYLY

God moves in a mysterious way
His wonders to perform;
He plants His footsteps in the sea,
And rides upon the storm.

WILLIAM COWPER

He made you so you could share in His creation,
could love and laugh and know Him.

TED GRIFFEN

....

For we are God's workmanship,
created in Christ Jesus to do good works,
which God prepared in advance for us to do.

EPHESIANS 2:10 NIV

....

Make a Difference

We must not, in trying to think about how we can make a big difference, ignore the small daily differences we can make which, over time, add up to big differences that we often cannot foresee.

MARIAN WRIGHT EDELMAN

If I can do some good today,
If I can serve along life's way,
If I can something helpful say,
Lord, show me how.

GRENVILLE KLEISER

There's nothing intrinsically wrong with ambition—Jesus often appealed to it— but the nature of those ambitions makes a huge difference: "He that would be chief among you must be servant of all."

ELISABETH ELLIOT

Everybody can be great...because anybody
can serve. You don't have to have a college degree
to serve.... You only need a heart full of grace.
A soul generated by love.

MARTIN LUTHER KING JR.

Our Lord does not care so much
for the importance of our works as for
the love with which they are done.

TERESA OF AVILA

Love keeps the cold out better than a cloak.
It serves for food and raiment.

HENRY WADSWORTH LONGFELLOW

....

Make the most of every opportunity.
Be gracious in your speech.
The goal is to bring out the best in others.

COLOSSIANS 4:5 MSG

....

Family Faces

There is nothing higher and stronger and more
wholesome and useful for life in later years
than some good memory, especially a memory
connected with childhood, with home.

FYODOR DOSTOYEVSKY

Our sweetest experiences of affection
are meant to point us to that realm which is
the real and endless home of the heart.

HENRY WARD BEECHER

Home is the bottom line of life, the anvil
upon which attitudes and convictions
are hammered out—the single most
influential force in our earthly existence.
No price tag can adequately reflect its value.

CHARLES SWINDOLL

Family faces are magic mirrors.
Looking at people who belong to us,
we see the past, present, and future.

GAIL LUMET BUCKLEY

We are so very rich if we know just a few
people in a way in which we know no others.

CATHERINE BRAMWELL-BOOTH

What families have in common the world around
is that they are the place where people learn
who they are and how to be that way.

JEAN ILLSLEY CLARKE

....

*Most of all, love each other
as if your life depended on it.
Love makes up for practically anything.*

1 PETER 4:8 MSG

....

Step of Faith

Faith means being sure of what we hope for...now.
It means knowing something is real, this moment,
all around you, even when you don't see it.
Great faith isn't the ability to believe
long and far into the misty future.
It's simply taking God at His word
and taking the next step.

JONI EARECKSON TADA

Faith expects from God what is
beyond all expectations.

If it can be verified, we don't need faith....
Faith is for that which lies on the other side
of reason. Faith is what makes life bearable,
with all its tragedies and ambiguities
and sudden, startling joys.

MADELEINE L'ENGLE

In the end, I think this is what women truly desire:
to know God and to stand tall in their faith,
strong at the core, tender in heart.

RUTH SENTER

Faith is not an effort, a striving,
a ceaseless seeking, as so many earnest
souls suppose, but rather a letting go,
an abandonment, an abiding rest in God
that nothing, not even the soul's
shortcomings, can disturb.

....

Let love and faithfulness never leave you;
bind them around your neck,
write them on the tablet of your heart.

PROVERBS 3:3 NIV

....

You Are a Blessing

We don't have to be perfect to be a blessing.
We are asked only to be real, trusting
in His perfection to cover our imperfection,
knowing that one day we will finally be
all that Christ saved us for
and wants us to be.

GIGI GRAHAM TCHIVIDJIAN

When seeds of kindness are sown prayerfully
in the garden plot of our lives, we may be sure
that there will be a bountiful harvest of
blessings for both us and others.

W. PHILLIP KELLER

Some blessings—like rainbows after rain or
a friend's listening ear—are extraordinary gifts
waiting to be discovered in an ordinary day.

Remember you are very special to God as His
precious child. He has promised to complete
the good work He has begun in you.
As you continue to grow in Him,
He will teach you to be a blessing to others.

GARY SMALLEY AND JOHN TRENT

May your footsteps set you upon
a lifetime of love.
May you wake each day with His blessings
and sleep each night in His keeping,
and may you always walk
in His tender care

....

I will bless you and make your name great,
and you will be a blessing.

GENESIS 12:2 NIV

....

Be Still and Know

Perhaps this moment is unclear, but let it be—
even if the next, and many moments after that
are unclear, let them be. Trust that God will
help you work them out, and that all the
unclear moments will bring you to that moment
of clarity and action when you are known by
Him and know Him. These are the better
and brighter moments of His blessing.

WENDY MOORE

We must concentrate on knowing God;
the more we know Him the more we
want to know Him. And as knowledge is
commonly the measure of love,
the deeper and wider our knowledge,
the greater will be our love.

BROTHER LAWRENCE

Commit your way to the LORD;
trust in him and he will do this:
He will make your righteousness
shine like the dawn, the justice of
your cause like the noonday sun.
Be still before the LORD
and wait patiently for him.

PSALM 37:5–7 NIV

Be still, and in the quiet moments,
listen to the voice of your heavenly Father.
His words can renew your spirit...no one
knows you and your needs like He does.

JANET L. SMITH

. . . .

Be still, and know that I am God!

PSALM 46:10 NLT

. . . .

In His Presence

I have been away and come back again many
times to this place. Each time I approach,
I regret ever having left. There is a peace here,
a serenity, even before I enter. Just the idea
of returning becomes a balm for the wounds
I've collected elsewhere. Before I can finish
even one knock, the door opens wide
and I am in His presence.

BARBARA FARMER

As we practice the presence of God,
more and more we find ourselves going
through the stresses and strains of daily
activity with an ease and serenity that
amazes even us...especially us.

RICHARD J. FOSTER

It is not objective proof of God's existence that
we want but the experience of God's presence.
That is the miracle we are really after, and
that is also, I think, the miracle that we really get.

FREDERICK BUECHNER

A living, loving God can and does make
His presence felt, can and does speak to us in
the silence of our hearts, can and does warm
and caress us till we no longer doubt
that He is near, that He is here.

BRENNAN MANNING

....

*You have made known to me the path of life;
you will fill me with joy in your presence.*

PSALM 16:11 NIV

....

Source of Beauty

Beauty puts a face on God.
When we gaze at nature, at a loved one,
at a work of art, our soul immediately
recognizes and is drawn to the face of God.

MARGARET BROWNLEY

Late have I loved You,
O beauty so ancient and so new.
Late have I loved You!
You were within me while I
have gone outside to seek You.
Unlovely myself, I rushed towards
all those lovely things You had made.
And always You were with me.

AUGUSTINE

There's not a tint that paints the rose
Or decks the lily fair,
Or marks the humblest flower that grows,
But God has placed it there....
There's not a place on earth's vast round,
In ocean's deep or air,
Where love and beauty are not found,
For God is everywhere.

The wonder of living is held within the beauty
of silence, the glory of sunlight...the sweetness of
fresh spring air, the quiet strength of earth,
and the love that lies at the very root of all things.

....

*Your beauty and love chase after me
every day of my life. I'm back home in the
house of GOD for the rest of my life.*

PSALM 23:6 MSG

....

Simply Be

Women of adventure have conquered their fates
and know how to live exciting and fulfilling lives
right where they are. They have learned to
reinvent themselves and find creative ways
to enjoy the world and their place in it.
They know how to take mini-vacations,
stop and smell the roses,
and live fully in the moment.

BARBARA JENKINS

For I have learned to be content whatever the
circumstances. I know what it is to be in need,
and I know what it is to have plenty.
I have learned the secret of being content in any
and every situation, whether well fed or hungry,
whether living in plenty or in want.

PHILIPPIANS 4:11–12 NIV

Where the soul is full of peace and joy,
outward surroundings and circumstances
are of comparatively little account.

HANNAH WHITALL SMITH

An unhurried sense of time
is in itself a form of wealth.

BONNIE FRIEDMAN

Let the day suffice, with all its joys and failings,
its little triumphs and defeats. I'd happily,
if sleepily, welcome evening as a time of rest,
and let it slip away, losing nothing.

KATHLEEN NORRIS

....

*If you're content to simply be yourself,
your life will count for plenty.*

MATTHEW 23:11 MSG

....

Fill Me Up

When I am in solitude, the presence of God is
so real and so full that there is nothing else I want.
The people I love are with me in God's presence,
beyond the surface choppiness of all the stresses
that separate us as finite beings on this earth,
and I am able to experience our ultimate
togetherness in God. This experience is absolutely
the only thing that fills the longing of my heart.

RUTH HALEY BARTON

God's love is like a river springing up
in the Divine Substance and flowing endlessly
through His creation, filling all things
with life and goodness and strength.

THOMAS MERTON

Our love to God arises out of our emptiness;
God's love to us out of His fullness.

HANNAH MORE

Prayer is to the spirit what breath is to the body. We treat prayer as though it were the spice of life, but the Bible prescribes it as a vital staple in our diet.

DAVID HUBBARD

Solitude is for those with an ample interior, with room to roam, well-provided with supplies. And I need a day or two, every so often, to make the journey.

CATHERINE CALVERT

·······················

The LORD will...satisfy your needs in a sun-scorched land.... You will be like a well-watered garden.

ISAIAH 58:11 NIV

·······················

Promise of Peace

I will let God's peace infuse every part of today.
As the chaos swirls and life's demands
pull at me on all sides, I will breathe in
God's peace that surpasses all understanding.
He has promised that He would set within me
a peace too deeply planted to be affected by
unexpected or exhausting demands.

God has not promised sun without rain,
joy without sorrow, peace without pain.
But God has promised strength for the day,
rest for the labor, light for the way,
grace for the trials, help from above,
unfailing sympathy, undying love.

ANNIE JOHNSON FLINT

Tarry at the promise till God meets you there.
He always returns by way of His promises.

L. B. COWMAN

All the way my Savior leads me—
What have I to ask beside?
Can I doubt His tender mercy,
Who through life has been my guide?
Heavenly peace, divinest comfort,
Here by faith in Him to dwell!
For I know, what'er befall me,
Jesus doeth all things well.

FANNY J. CROSBY

. . . .

*The peace of God, which transcends all
understanding, will guard your hearts
and your minds in Christ Jesus.*

PHILIPPIANS 4:7 NIV

. . . .

A True Friend

Having someone who understands is a great
blessing for ourselves. Being someone
who understands is a great blessing to others.

JANETTE OKE

A true friend is one who is concerned about
what we are becoming, who sees beyond
the present relationship and cares deeply
about us as a whole person.

GLORIA GAITHER

To have a friend is to have one of the
sweetest gifts that life can bring;
to be a friend is to have a solemn and
tender education of soul from day to day.

AMY ROBERTSON BROWN

When you are truly joined in spirit,
another woman's good is your good too.
Your work for the good of each other.

RUTH SENTER

If we would build on a sure foundation in
friendship, we must love friends for
their sake rather than for our own.

CHARLOTTE BRONTË

Friendship is the fruit gathered from the trees
planted in the rich soil of love,
and nurtured with tender care and understanding.

ALMA L. WEIXELBAUM

Insomuch as anyone pushes you nearer to God,
he or she is your friend.

FRENCH PROVERB

....

*Perfume and incense bring joy to the heart,
and the pleasantness of one's friend
springs from his earnest counsel.*

PROVERBS 27:9 NIV

....

Investing in Prayer

Prayer is such an ordinary, everyday,
mundane thing. Certainly, people who
pray are no more saints than the rest of us.
Rather, they are people who want to
share a life with God, to love and be loved,
to speak and to listen, to work
and to be at rest in the presence of God.

ROBERTA BONDI

How vital that we pray, armed with the knowledge
that God is in heaven. Pray with any lesser conviction
and your prayers are timid, shallow, and hollow.
But spend some time walking in the workshop of
the heavens, seeing what God has done,
and watch how your prayers are energized.

MAX LUCADO

We must take our troubles to the Lord,
but we must do more than that;
we must leave them there.

HANNAH WHITALL SMITH

There isn't a certain time we
should set aside to talk about God.
God is part of our every waking moment.

MARVA COLLINS

When we call on God, He bends
down His ear to listen, as a father
bends down to listen to his little child.

ELIZABETH CHARLES

....

*Devote yourselves to prayer with an
alert mind and a thankful heart.*

COLOSSIANS 4:2 NLT

....

Imagine That

I still find each day too short for all the thoughts
I want to think, all the walks I want to take,
all the books I want to read, and all the friends
I want to see. The longer I live, the more my mind
dwells upon the beauty and the wonder of the world.

JOHN BURROUGHS

Isn't it a wonderful morning?
The world looks like something God
had just imagined for His own pleasure.

LUCY MAUD MONTGOMERY

The patterns of our days are always changing...
rearranging...and each design for living is unique...
graced with its own special beauty.

In all ranks of life the human heart
yearns for the beautiful, and the beautiful
things that God makes are His gift to all alike.

HARRIET BEECHER STOWE

Stand outside this evening. Look at the stars.
Know that you are special and loved
by the One who created them.

The moment you begin to delight in beauty,
your heart and mind are raised.

BASIL HUME

....

God can do anything, you know—
far more than you could ever imagine
or guess or request in your wildest dreams!

EPHESIANS 3:20 MSG

....

A Heart of Wisdom

I am convinced beyond a shadow of any doubt
that the most valuable pursuit
we can embark upon is to know God.

KAY ARTHUR

Tune your ears to wisdom,
and concentrate on understanding.
Cry out for insight,
and ask for understanding.
Search for them as you would for silver;
seek them like hidden treasures.
Then you will understand
what it means to fear the LORD,
and you will gain knowledge of God.

PROVERBS 2:2–5 NLT

Wisdom from God shows itself
most clearly in a loving heart.

LLOYD JOHN OGILVIE

This voice that calls to us out of the everyday
moments of life is called the wisdom of God.
This wisdom is infused into nature and the
laws that govern her, and into human nature
and the laws that govern it.

KEN GIRE

What we need is not new light, but new sight;
not new paths, but new strength
to walk in the old ones;
not new duties but new wisdom from on High
to fulfill those that are plain before us.

Kindness is more important than wisdom, and
the recognition of this is the beginning of wisdom.

THEODORE ISAAC RUBIN

....

*Teach us to number our days aright,
that we may gain a heart of wisdom.*

PSALM 90:12 NIV

....

Fountain of Beauty

Has anyone by fussing before the mirror
ever gotten taller by so much as an inch?
If fussing can't even do that, why fuss at all?
Walk into the fields and look at the wildflowers.
They don't fuss with their appearance—
but have you ever seen color and design quite
like it? The ten best-dressed men and women
in the country look shabby alongside them.
If God gives such attention to the wildflowers,
most of them never even seen, don't you
think he'll attend to you, take pride
in you, do his best for you?

LUKE 12:25–28 MSG

Beauty is the radiance of truth,
the fragrance of goodness.

VINCENT MCNABB

The fountain of beauty is the heart,
and every generous thought
illustrates the walls of your chamber.

FRANCIS QUARLES

Nothing can compare to the beauty and
greatness of the soul in which our King dwells
in His full majesty. No earthly fire can compare
with the light of its blazing love.
No bastions can compare with
its ability to endure forever.

TERESA OF AVILA

. . . .

*God has made everything beautiful
for its own time. He has planted
eternity in the human heart.*

ECCLESIASTES 3:11 NLT

. . . .

Extra in the Ordinary

In ordinary life we hardly realize that we receive
a great deal more than we give, and that
it is only with gratitude that life becomes rich.

DIETRICH BONHOEFFER

Every day we live is a priceless gift of God,
loaded with possibilities to learn something new,
to gain fresh insights.

DALE EVANS ROGERS

Simplicity will enable you to leap lightly.
Increasingly you will find yourself living in
a state of grace, finding...the sacred in the
ordinary, the mystical in the mundane.

DAVID YOUNT

Take your everyday, ordinary life—
your sleeping, eating, going-to-work, and
walking-around life—and place it
before God as an offering.

ROMANS 12:1 MSG

The incredible gift of the ordinary!
Glory comes streaming from the table of daily life.

MACRINA WIEDERKEHR

God has always used ordinary people
to carry out His extraordinary mission.

We are not called by God to extraordinary
things, but to do ordinary things
with extraordinary love.

JEAN VANIER

God still draws near to us in the ordinary,
commonplace, everyday experiences and places....
He comes in surprising ways.

HENRY GARIEPY

. . . .

*We carry this precious Message around in
the unadorned clay pots of our ordinary lives.*

2 CORINTHIANS 4:7 MSG

. . . .

Gifts to Share

This is the real gift: you have been given
the breath of life, designed with a unique,
one-of-a-kind soul that exists forever—
the way that you choose to live it
doesn't change the fact that you've been given
the gift of being now and forever.
Priceless in value, you are handcrafted by God,
who has a personal design and plan for each of us.

WENDY MOORE

When I stand before God at the end of my life,
I would hope that I would not have a
single bit of talent left and could say,
"I used everything You gave me."

ERMA BOMBECK

Lord...give me the gift of faith to be renewed
and shared with others each day. Teach me to live
this moment only, looking neither to the past
with regret, nor the future with apprehension.
Let love be my aim and my life a prayer.

ROSEANN ALEXANDER-ISHAM

God gave me my gifts. I will do all I can
to show Him how grateful I am to Him.

GRACE LIVINGSTON HILL

. . . .

Well done, good and faithful servant;
you were faithful over a few things,
I will make you ruler over many things.
Enter into the joy of your lord.

MATTHEW 25:21 NKJV

. . . .

Faithful Promises

Commit to hope. There's reason to!
For the believer, hope is divinely assured
things that aren't here yet! Our hope is
grounded in unshakable promises.

JACK HAYFORD

Our feelings do not affect God's facts.
They may blow up, like clouds, and cover the
eternal things that we do most truly believe.
We may not see the shining of the promises—
but they still shine!

AMY CARMICHAEL

Faith in God is not blind. It is based on
His character and His promises.

If you are seeking after God, you may be
sure of this: God is seeking you much more.
He is the Lover, and you are His beloved.
He has promised Himself to you.

JOHN OF THE CROSS

Faithful, O Lord, Thy mercies are,
A rock that cannot move!
A thousand promises declare
Thy constancy of love.

CHARLES WESLEY

Faith involves waiting on a promise.
Our hope is based on a promise.
God promised He would be "with us,"
not as an unseen ethereal force, but in the
form of a person with a name: Jesus.

MICHAEL CARD

God makes a promise—faith believes it,
hope anticipates it, patience quietly awaits it.

....

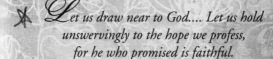

*Let us draw near to God.... Let us hold
unswervingly to the hope we profess,
for he who promised is faithful.*

HEBREWS 10:22–23 NIV

....

An Invitation

If you have ever:

    questioned if this is all there is to life...

    wondered what happens when you die...

    felt a longing for purpose or significance...

    wrestled with resurfacing anger...

    struggled to forgive someone...

    known there is a "higher power" but couldn't define it...

    sensed you have a role to play in the world...

    experienced success and still felt empty afterward...

then consider Jesus.

A great teacher from two millennia ago, Jesus of Nazareth, the Son of God, freely chose to show our Maker's everlasting love for us by offering to take all of our flaws, darkness, death, and mistakes into His very body (1 Peter 2:24). The result was His death on a cross. But the story doesn't end there. God raised Him from the dead and invites us to believe this truth in our hearts and follow Jesus into eternal life.

If you confess with your mouth that Jesus is Lord and believe in your heart that God raised him from the dead, you will be saved. —ROMANS 10:9